Dear

Dear Newlyweds

Also from Charles McEnerney & Adam Larson:

Dear Graduate

A book for when we take a step forward.

Dear Love

A book about being together.

Dear Newlyweds

A book to take with you from this day forward.

Charles McEnerney & Adam Larson

Clarkson Potter/Publishers
New York

Clarkson Potter/Publishers
An imprint of the Crown Publishing Group
A division of Penguin Random House LLC
1745 Broadway
New York, NY 10019
clarksonpotter.com
penguinrandomhouse.com

Library of Congress Cataloging-in-Publication Data is on file with the publisher.

ISBN 979-8-217-03534-2
Ebook ISBN 979-8-217-03535-9

Editor: Emma Brodie | Assistant editor: Briana James
Designer: Adam Larson | Art director: Ian Dingman
Production editor: Leni Schenkel | Production: Kim Tyner, Dan Myers

Manufactured in India

10 9 8 7 6 5 4 3 2 1

First Edition

The authorized representative in the EU for product safety and compliance is Penguin Random House Ireland, Morrison Chambers, 32 Nassau Street, Dublin D02 YH68, Ireland, https://eu-contact.penguin.ie.

For Christopher & Burcu, Joseph & Cara,
Kaitlin & Abbey, Katie, Kerry & Kevin, Lucas & Kayla, Jackson,
Maura & Adam, Meghan & Dan, Phoenix, Reid, River, Sean,
Shane, and Zach

Congratulations!

You have found the person you want to be with forever.

Someone who makes
you laugh, who
makes you feel safe,
and who makes you
feel seen and heard.

You have found
your "better half,"
your best friend.

The first person you want to tell when something good happens.

And the first person
you want to tell
when something
bad happens, too.

You've opened your hearts and decided to commit to each other.

You've promised to love, cherish, and support each other, forever.

To be there for each other for better or worse, for richer or poorer, in sickness and in health, until death do you part.

To have and to hold, from this day forward.

But sometimes these vows don't make sense until later.

Because life is
an unpredictable
adventure.

Over time,
marriage will
come to mean many
different things.

Your bond will
be your compass
to navigate whatever
lies ahead.

As you face
new challenges,
you will be asked
new questions.

Will you grow together, in parallel, strengthening that bond over time?

Will you strive
to be honest
and kind to
one another?

Will you find ways to love even each other's faults?

Will you push
each other to reach
for big goals
and provide the
encouragement
needed to
achieve them?

Will you lead
with compassion,
consoling each
other through pain,
grief, or loss?

Will you do your best to communicate clearly, remembering that no one can read minds?

Will you celebrate every win, big and small?

Will you help each other become the best versions of yourselves?

Will you be a team, a true partnership, championing each other's strengths?

Will you lift each
other up, even on
days when you
are really down?

Will you be the
spirit of hope in the
face of unexpected
hardship?

Will you remain intimate in body, mind, and spirit?

Will you remain faithful to and respect each other's needs, wants, and desires?

Will you catch
each other
when you fall?

One day, you will look back on the beginning of your marriage.

You will build upon your wedding day with a lifetime of days.

You will have funny stories about impossible times that you will eventually laugh about.

You will create a family—biological, chosen, or both—that will fill you with love and purpose.

You will look back at all the things you felt together, learned together, and survived together.

No matter what comes your way, always remember your love.

Remember that vulnerability is your superpower.

Remember how
strong you are
as individuals,
but that you are
stronger together.

Remember those three little words you can never say enough.

And remember all the reasons you said "I do."

Charles McEnerney

Charles McEnerney is a writer, musician, marketer and, most importantly, a dad to Adacie and Declan. He is the co-author of *Dear Graduate* and *Dear Love*. Throughout his career, he has worked at HBO, GBH/PBS, *Fast Company* and *MovieMaker* magazines, Emerson College, The Grommet, and 826 Boston. Charlie was the singer/songwriter in the post-punk band Falling Stairs and is now a solo artist. Charlie grew up in Flushing, Queens, and lives in Jamaica Plain in Boston, MA. If he's not writing, he is likely listening to music, playing music, reading, watching the news, or with Adam in a bookstore looking for a book he doesn't have room for at home. **charlesmcenerney.com**

Adam Larson

Adam Larson is an award-winning creative director, designer, artist, and illustrator. He is the co-author of *Dear Graduate* and *Dear Love*. He is the founder of the multidisciplinary brand design studio Adam&Co., whose clients have included Beyoncé, Taylor Swift, Herbie Hancock, Hoka, Nike, Puma, Saucony, Converse, The Boston Public Library, Harvard, NYU, MIT, CNN, ESPN, Penguin Books, and Random House, among others. He is the co-founding editor and art director of *Lemon* and *Wednesday* magazines. He has taught design at MassArt and currently lives in Florence, MA. If he's not doting on his American Bully, Rhys, he is likely reading; at a gallery, museum, or bookstore; or riding his bike with Charlie down Commercial Street in Provincetown. **adamnco.com**

Thank You

Barbara Daly, Adacie McEnerney, Declan McEnerney,
Vilma & John McEnerney, Maureen McGrath,
Emma Brodie at Clarkson Potter,
and Kristin van Ogtrop at InkWell Management and their teams
for all of your support!

And thank you to all of the bookstores and gift shops
that carried our books, *Dear Graduate* and *Dear Love*!